Bobby and Billy
A TALE OF TWO HOMES

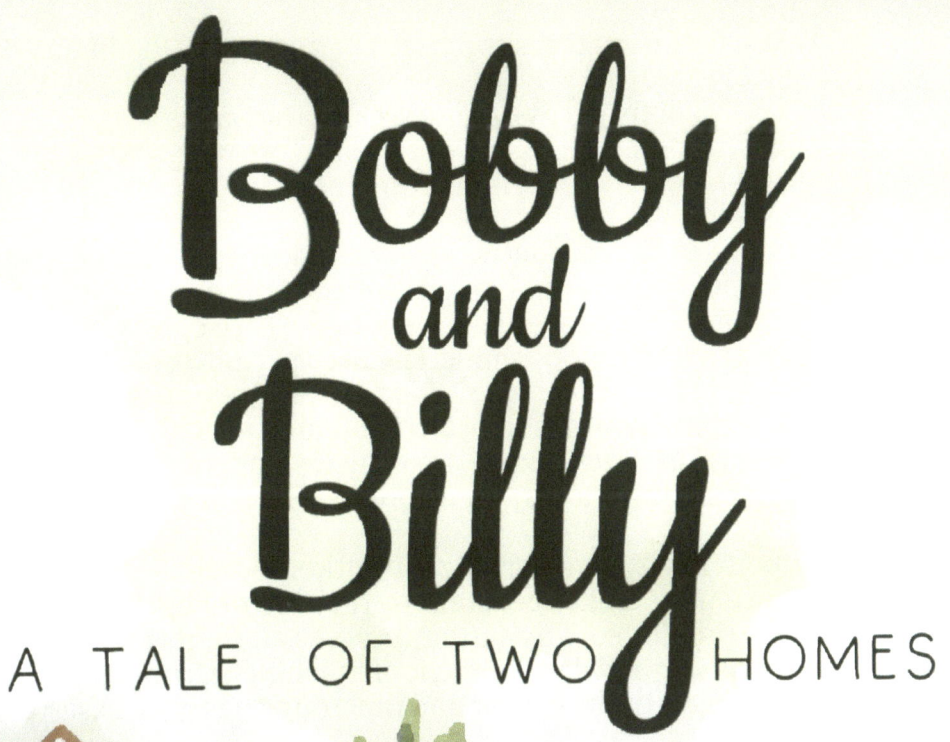

SUZY RIEDMAN

Text and Illustrations copyright © 2025 Suzy Riedman

Published by Family Wealth Dynamics

All rights reserved.

No part of this publication may be reproduced, distributed, or transmitted in any form or by any means, including photocopying, recording, or other electronic or mechanical methods, without the prior written permission of the publisher, except in the case of brief quotations embodied in reviews and certain other noncommercial uses permitted by copyright law.

This book is a work of fiction. Names, characters, and incidents are either the product of the author's imagination or are used fictitiously, and any resemblance to actual persons living or dead, business establishments, events, or locales is entirely coincidental.

NO AI TRAINING: Without in any way limiting the author's exclusive rights under copyright, any use of this publication to "train" generative artificial intelligence (AI) technologies to generate text is expressly prohibited. The author reserves all rights to license uses of this work for generative AI training and development of machine learning language models.
The moral right of the author and illustrator has been asserted.

Cover design and illustrations by
Hardback ISBN-13: 978-1-969667-01-5
Paperback ISBN-13: 978-1-969667-00-8
eBook ISBN-13: 978-1-969667-02-2
Library of Congress Control Number:
Riedman, Suzy

Bobby and Billy: A Tale of Two Homes / Suzy Riedman

Bobby and Billy are best friends from opposite ends of the socioeconomic spectrum. When Billy visits Bobby's house, he is both amazed and envious of all Bobby's nice toys and enormous property. Bobby and Billy both have loving homes, and they learn that a happy life is not about having nice things and big houses but about appreciating what you have.

ISBN-(hc) 13:

DEDICATION

To Chris and Bo—Two guys who know how to be happy.

Bobby and Billy are best friends.

"Wanna come over and play?" invited Bobby.

Billy arrives at Bobby's house. His mom has to press numbers on a keypad to open a big gate.

Bobby can't wait to see Billy. He runs all the way to the gate to race Billy's car back up to the house.

"Bobby, your house is huge!" Billy exclaims.

"Yeah!" Bobby says. "Come see my room! I have a teenager bed!"

Bobby and Billy sprint through the house, and Bobby dives onto his bed.

Billy stands still and looks around. "Are all these toys yours?" he asks with wide eyes.

"Yep!" Bobby says proudly. "This is my ukulele." He strums a few strings. "This is my bookshelf, and these are my books. And this is my chair. And this is the dresser my grandpa made. And this is my collection of stuffed animals. This is Tyga, he's my favorite."

He hugs a big stuffed tiger.

Bobby shows Billy around. There's a cat room, a dog room, a guest room, his mom and dad's room, their offices, four bathrooms, the TV room, and a room Bobby's parents call "great."

This room is filled with nice furniture. It has high ceilings and big windows that look out over a pasture of horses.

Bobby loves his home.

Bobby leads the way to his favorite room: the playroom. Billy trails close behind.

"Watch this!" Bobby puts a miniature sports car on the race track. It speeds through the loops.

"Wow!" Billy says, impressed by all Bobby's toys.

"I wish I had a playroom!" Bobby's house is really neat, and Billy feels a little jealous of all his fast cars and big rooms.

Bobby and Billy build a big tower with magnetic blocks and knock it down with remote-controlled monster trucks.

They ride around on Bobby's ATV.

They jump on the trampoline and feed carrots to the horses.

On the way home, Billy says, "Bobby has so many fun toys and such a big house! I wish I had an ATV and a big pasture to drive it in."

Billy's family has a small house.

Billy and his brother share a room with a bunk bed and a toy chest full of pre-loved toys that were passed down from other kids.

Billy's sisters also share a room with a bunk bed and a table piled high with projects.

Billy's house has one bathroom for showering and a guest bathroom, where he brushes his teeth every night.

Wally, the family dog, lives in their small fenced yard. There is a garden, a picnic table, and lots of daisies in the spring.

"You're right, Billy," his mom says. "Bobby has a lot of nice things. Does seeing what he has make it hard to appreciate what you have?"

Billy shrugs. "I guess," he mumbles.

Billy thinks about this as he steps inside.

The smell of warm cookies greets him. The family photos surround him, feeling like a warm hug.

Billy sees the wood by the fireplace, where he and his dad build fires together.

He hears his brother and sisters playing in the backyard. There is laughter and joy all around him.

Billy's dad walks in, whistling. He has a hammer in his hand. "Do you want to help me fix a hole in the fence?" he asks Billy.

Billy is very good at fixing things. He grabs a hammer and follows his dad outside with a smile on his face.

Happiness doesn't come from having the most— it comes from loving what you have. This is his home and family, and he wouldn't have it any other way.

Billy loves his home.

Conversation Prompts

1. Bobby has lots of toys, and Billy doesn't have as many. Do you think that makes one of them richer than the other? Why or why not?

2. What are some things money can buy? What are some things money can't buy?

3. If you had $10, what would you do with it? Spend it, save it, share it—or something else?

4. Can you think of a time when having something new made you happy for a little while, but the feeling didn't last?

5. What are some things in your life that make you feel "rich" even though they don't cost any money?

6. What do you think is the purpose of money? How do you think it can be used in good ways?

7. Who are the people in your life that make you feel loved, safe, and happy? How is that a kind of wealth?

ABOUT THE AUTHOR

Suzy Riedman is a writer, coach, mediator, and real estate investor who has always loved finding creative ways to earn and discuss money. She holds a bachelor's degree in creative writing from the University of Redlands.

Suzy's love for honest money conversations began when she was ten years old and saved up to buy a cash register. She ran an office supply store out of her bedroom - selling envelopes, stamps and pencils she'd found on her parents' desks. After college, Suzy lived in Hawaii and worked as a personal trainer and Crossfit coach before returning to Oregon and entering the world of real estate investing and financial independence.

Inspired by her own journey of taking ownership of her financial life, Suzy writes books to help families start money conversations that are engaging, age-appropriate, and meaningful. Her goal is to give kids confidence about earning, saving, and using money—while giving parents the tools to guide them.

Suzy lives on a little farm with her family, a menagerie of animals including a trick horse named Whistle, and 46 very busy chickens. When she isn't writing, Suzy can be found riding bikes with her husband and son, hiking, or hanging out in the barn.